Exper

EARTH SCIENCE AND WEATHER

with Toys and Everyday Stuff

BY EMILY SOHN

Raintree is an imprint of Capstone Global Library Limited, a company incorporated in England and Wales having its registered office at 7 Pilgrim Street, London, EC4V 6LB – Registered company number: 6695582

www.raintree.co.uk
myorders@raintree.co.uk

Edited by Alesha Sullivan
Designed by Kyle Grenz
Picture research by Jo Miller
Production by Kathy McColley

ISBN 978 1 474 70357 4 (hardback)
19 18 17 16 15
10 9 8 7 6 5 4 3 2 1

ISBN 978 1 474 70362 8 (paperback)
20 19 18 17 16
10 9 8 7 6 5 4 3 2 1

British Library Cataloguing in Publication Data
A full catalogue record for this book is available from the British Library.

Acknowledgements
Capstone Studio/Karon Dubke except: Nova Development Corporation, 19 (globes); Shutterstock: Merkushev Vasiliy, 8 (water cycle), MichaelJayBerlin, cover (push pins), Nitr, cover (towels), Petr Malyshev, cover (flashlight)

We would like to thank Paul Ohmann, PhD, Associate Professor of Physics at the University of St. Thomas in St. Paul, Minnesota, for his invaluable help in the preparation of this book.

Every effort has been made to contact copyright holders of material reproduced in this book. Any omissions will be rectified in subsequent printings if notice is given to the publisher.

All the internet addresses (URLs) given in this book were valid at the time of going to press. However, due to the dynamic nature of the internet, some addresses may have changed, or sites may have changed or ceased to exist since publication. While the author and publisher regret any inconvenience this may cause readers, no responsibility for any such changes can be accepted by either the author or the publisher.

Printed and Bound in China

CONTENTS

TURN YOUR HOUSE INTO A SCIENCE LAB!

Weather on Earth affects us every day. Sun, wind, rain or snow can change what we do and what we wear. Will we be cold? Will we get wet? Can we play at the park?

Some types of weather can also be dangerous, such as tornadoes or thunderstorms. Have a look around your house and gather some materials. Then use them to learn all about weather and science with some fantastic experiments!

Safety first!

You may need an adult's help for some of these experiments. But most of them can be done on your own. If you have a question about how to do a step safely, make sure you ask an adult. Think safety first!

TURN TO PAGE 20 TO SEE HOW THE SCIENCE WORKS IN EACH EXPERIMENT!

5

LET IT RAIN

Tiny water droplets in warm air cause rain to fall from the clouds. Rain helps plants and trees grow and fills lakes and rivers. But how does water get inside clouds? All you need is a bathroom and some toys to find out!

Materials:

2 plastic toys, like these action figures

bathroom with a shower

2 rubber toys, such as a duck or ball

2 metal toys, like these cars

Steps:

1. Ask an adult to help you turn on the shower. Make the water as hot as it will go.

2. Close the door to the room. Close all windows. Turn off any fans.

3. Put one of each kind of toy on the floor. Put the others up high on a cupboard or ledge.

4. When the bathroom is full of steam, turn the shower off. Are any of the toys wet? How did they get water on them?

5. There should be mist on the mirror. Use your finger to draw a picture or write your name. Does your finger feel wet?

THE WATER CYCLE

Think about the huge size of our planet. Did you know that water covers over 70 per cent of Earth? Water fills oceans, lakes and the ground under your feet. It falls from the sky as **precipitation**. But before it can rain or snow, water has to **evaporate**. Use some flannels to see how evaporation works!

Materials: 3 identical flannels

Ongoing cycle

Evaporation moves the water from lakes and puddles into the sky. Then water falls from the sky as rain or snow. This is called the water cycle.

Steps:

1. In a sink soak all of the flannels. Then squeeze out any extra water.

2. Hang one wet flannel in the sunshine outside. Hang one in the shade outside. Hang the last one in the bathroom inside your house.

3. Check the flannels every 10 minutes. Which one dries first? Which takes the longest to dry? Where has the water gone?

precipitation water that falls from the clouds in the form of rain, hail or snow
evaporate change from a liquid to a gas

THE BEAUTY OF RAINBOWS

Rainbows are pretty! They can also teach us about light and weather. As sunlight goes through a raindrop, the light is sorted into rainbow colours. You may know the colours of the rainbow – red, orange, yellow, green, blue, indigo and violet.

You can create a rainbow in your house too! Use a glass of water to sort light into colours.

Materials:

water

clear glass

a piece of white paper

Why is the sky blue?

The air is full of dust and other specks. Sunlight bounces off these specks. On a colour **spectrum**, blue light spreads out the best. So on a clear day, we see a blue sky.

Steps:

1. **Put a piece of paper in front of a window on a ledge or table.**

2. **Fill a clear glass with water. The water should be about 2.5 centimetres (1 inch) from the top of the glass.** ●·····················●

3. **Hold the glass just above the paper so that the sunlight can shine through it. Be careful not to spill any water! The rays of sunlight should hit the paper. The water bends the sunlight. What can you see on the paper? Can you see rainbow colours?** ●··················●

Tip:

You may need to move the glass or paper to get the light to hit just right.

spectrum range of colours that is shown when light shines through drops of water

BLOWN AWAY!

Wind can help you fly a kite. Wind can also move a sailing boat across the water. Wind comes from sunlight heating the **atmosphere**, causing air to flow. Make a pinwheel to learn more about the power of wind!

Materials:

pencil with eraser

drawing pin

ruler

thick, rectangular construction paper

pencil

small fan

scissors

Steps:

1. Draw a square using your pencil. Ask an adult to help you. Each side should be 10-centimetres (4-in) long. Then cut the square out of the construction paper. ● · ·

atmosphere mixture of gases that surrounds Earth

2. Cut towards the middle of the square from each corner. Make sure you don't cut all the way to the centre. Ask an adult to use a drawing pin to poke holes in the top corner of every other slit and one in the middle of the square.

3. Curl the corners with holes towards the middle. Ask an adult to push the pin through all five holes. Attach the pin to the pencil's eraser. Don't attach it too tightly. The pin needs to be able to spin freely.

4. Take your pinwheel outside or hold it in front of a fan. Does it spin? What happens if you turn the pinwheel sideways? How can you hold it to make the wheel spin the most quickly?

Fact:

Wind turbines work in a similar way to a pinwheel. Wind moves large blades that generate electricity to power nearby towns and cities.

TWISTER!

Underneath a dark thunderstorm, a thick **_funnel cloud_** forms. The wind inside of that cloud whips at speeds up to 300 miles (483 kilometres) per hour. It howls and spins. This is how a tornado begins! Tornadoes can destroy houses and topple trees. Use two empty bottles to make your own twister!

Materials:

strong tape, such as duct tape

2 empty 2-litre plastic bottles

water (blue food colouring is optional)

funnel cloud cone-shaped cloud that is usually a visible part of a tornado

Steps:

1. **Remove the tops from both bottles.**

2. **Pour water into one of the bottles. Fill the bottle more than half full but not all the way to the top. Leave the other bottle empty.** ●·············

3. **Turn the empty bottle upside down. Line it up with the other bottle so the openings meet. Tape the necks** ●·············· **together tightly.**

Tip:
Ask an adult to help you hold the two bottles together while you tape.

4. **Turn the bottles over. The bottle with water in it should be on the top. Quickly, give the bottles a little swirl. Look inside. Can you see a funnel that looks like a tornado?** ●·············

ELECTRIC SKY

There is **electricity** in the sky, especially during a storm. Electricity flows between clouds. Or it can flow between a cloud and the ground. This is known as **lightning**.

Lightning looks like a flash, and it sometimes fills the sky with bright light. Try to make some mini lightning of your own!

Materials:

scissors

aluminium cake tin

tape

flat piece of polystyrene, at least as big as your hand

Flying sparks!

There are other ways to make mini lightning bolts! Put socks on and shuffle your feet on a rug. Touch a metal object with one finger. Kazam! Prepare to feel a mini electric shock!

electricity movement of electrons that can be used to make light and heat or to make machines work

lightning electricity caused by friction in a cloud

Steps:

1. Ask an adult to help you use the scissors to cut a thin strip from the polystyrene.

2. Tape the strip of polystyrene to the inside of the cake tin. This will be the handle.

3. Rub the large piece of polystyrene all over your hair. Rub really quickly!

4. Put the large piece of polystyrene down on a table. The part that touched your hair should be face up.

5. Use the handle to pick up the cake tin. Hold it about 0.3 metre (1 foot) above the polystyrene, and let it drop.

6. Carefully touch the cake tin with the tip of your finger. Did you feel a spark?

17

SEASONAL DIFFERENCES

Is the weather hot or cold where you live? It could be both! We often plan our lives around seasons. Over the winter children often like to go sledging. In the summer it's common to go swimming to cool down.

As Earth spins, daytime changes to night-time. While the Earth spins, it also **orbits** the Sun. This orbiting tells us what time of the year it is. Use toys to learn more about seasons!

Materials:

washable marker

big yellow ball

small blue ball

Steps:

1. Place the yellow ball on a table. This is the Sun. ●

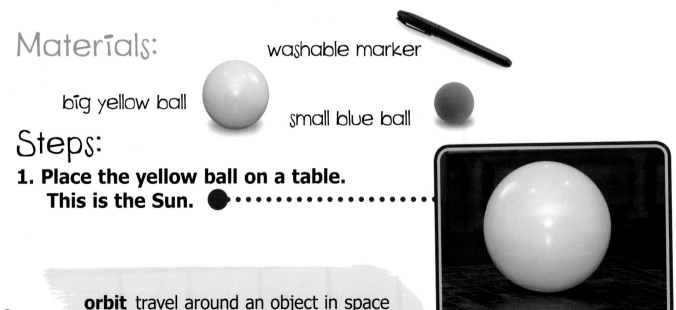

orbit travel around an object in space

18

2. **Draw a small dot on the blue ball. The blue ball is Earth, and the dot is the North Pole.**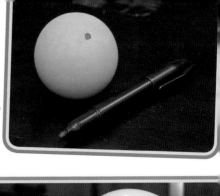

3. **Hold Earth so the North Pole is tilted towards the Sun. If you live on the northern half of Earth, this means it's summer. Your home faces the Sun.**

4. **Walk around the table so you're on the other side of the Sun. You are in orbit. Keep Earth leaning the same way. Now it is winter. Your home faces away from the Sun, and it's colder outside.**

5. **Pretend you live near the South Pole. How might the seasons differ from where you live now?**

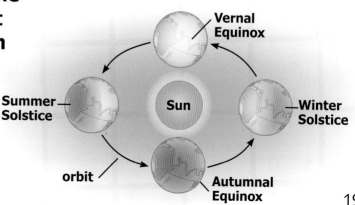

Vernal Equinox

Summer Solstice

Sun

Winter Solstice

orbit

Autumnal Equinox

WHY IT WORKS

Would you like to know how these amazing experiments work? Here is the science behind the fun!

PAGE 6 - LET IT RAIN

Steam is **water vapour** in the air. When the warm water touched the cool toys, it changed from gas form into a liquid.

PAGE 8 - THE WATER CYCLE

The flannel in the sunlight should have dried the quickest because of the Sun's heat. The Sun's heat made the water turn into a gas, which is known as evaporation.

PAGE 10 - THE BEAUTY OF RAINBOWS

Rainbows form when sunlight bends as it passes through drops of water. The light acted the same when it passed through your glass of water. The light was sorted into pretty rainbow colours.

PAGE 12 - BLOWN AWAY!

When the wind blows on the blades of your pinwheel, they spin. Wind is sometimes used to create clean power instead of using gas or oil to make electricity.

PAGE 14 - TWISTER!

In this experiment swirling the bottles forms a **vortex**, similar to spinning air in a system of thunderstorms.

PAGE 16 - ELECTRIC SKY

When you rubbed the polystyrene on your hair, you pulled **electrons** onto the piece of polystyrene. These electrons then moved onto the cake tin when they touched. When your finger touched the metal cake tin, some electrons created a mini spark of electricity.

PAGE 18 - SEASONAL DIFFERENCES

It takes six months for Earth to move from one side of the Sun to the opposite side. And it takes an entire year to go all the way around the Sun. When it is summer in the northern half of the world, it is winter in the southern half.

water vapour water in gas form
vortex air moving in a circular motion
electron one of the tiny particles that make up all things

GLOSSARY

atmosphere mixture of gases that surrounds Earth

electricity movement of electrons that can be used to make light and heat or to make machines work

electron one of the tiny particles that make up all things

evaporate change from a liquid to a gas

funnel cloud cone-shaped cloud that is usually a visible part of a tornado

lightning electricity caused by friction in a cloud

orbit travel around an object in space

precipitation water that falls from the clouds in the form of rain, hail or snow

spectrum range of colours that is shown when light shines through drops of water

vortex air moving in a circular motion

water vapour water in gas form

READ MORE

Experiments with Eletricity (Read and Experiment), Isabel Thomas (Raintree, 2015)

Liquid Planet (Discover Earth Science), Tammy Enz (Raintree, 2012)

Weather Infographics (Infographics), Chris Oxlade (Raintree, 2014)

WEBSITES

www.bbc.co.uk/schools/whatisweather/
Play some games and learn more about the key features of weather on Earth, including the Sun, temperature, precipitation and wind.

www.metoffice.gov.uk/learning/weather-for-kids
Explore the Met Office's 'Weather for kids' website to find more weather experiments, look at some extreme weather and learn more about how the weather affects Earth.

INDEX